D0372279

DEVELOPING
Better Athletes,
Better People

A Leader's Guide to Transforming High School and Youth Sports
into a Development Zone™

By Jim Thompson
Foreword by Doc Rivers

Balance Sports Publishing, LLC, Portola Valley, California

Balance Sports Publishing, LLC
195 Lucero Way
Portola Valley, CA 94028
(650) 561-9586

ISBN: 978-0-9821317-6-3

First Edition
Printed in the United States of America
10 9 8 7 6 5 4 3 2   17 16 15

Balance Sports Publishing, LLC and the author disclaim responsibility for adverse effects or consequences from the misapplication or injudicious use of the information contained in this book. Mention of resources and associations does not imply endorsement by Balance Sports Publishing, LLC or the author.

Book designed by Elisa Tanaka

This book is dedicated to the memory of my fierce and loving mother,
the first courageous leader in my life:
Marjorie Eileen Lorraine Score Thompson Bjerkager
May 17, 1921 – July 4, 2013

Table of Contents

Foreword
By Doc Rivers

I became a supporter of PCA after meeting Jim Thompson. I have seen both the good and bad of youth sports. In addition to my career as a player and coach, I have been a sports parent for my four children, some of whom competed through the college level.

The difference a coach can make in a youth's life is enormous, and PCA is showing high school and youth coaches how to be a Double-Goal Coach who teaches life lessons while preparing their team to win on the scoreboard.

That is why I am excited about this book. *Developing Better Athletes, Better People* shows how to create a culture that will support coaches in bringing out the best in their athletes.

I know from personal experience the power of culture. Basketball is the ultimate team game, and it is a team's culture that largely determines how well the individuals on the team work together.

Much of our success at the Boston Celtics was due to our creating a culture of "Ubuntu." Ubuntu is an African word that means, "I can't be all I can be unless you are all you can be."

This new book by Jim Thompson lays out a vision and practical tools for high school athletic directors and leaders of youth sports organizations to establish a culture to develop Better Athletes, Better People. That is a worthy goal, and I am proud to be part of the PCA Movement.

Doc Rivers
NBA Championship Coach

**There isn't any other youth institution that equals
sports as a setting in which to develop character.
There just isn't. Sports are the perfect setting because
character is tested all the time. It means a great deal
if that time is well used.**

John W. Gardner, Founder, Common Cause and
PCA National Advisory Board Founding Member

A Major Institution

Recently, I spoke at my 25th MBA reunion at the Stanford Graduate
School of Business about Positive Coaching Alliance. I said that making
sure kids have a good sports experience might not be as critical as ending
poverty or slowing climate disruption. But I had a lever to make a difference here, while I didn't with other big problems our society faced.

A classmate and longtime coach and sports parent, Mike Stanley, challenged me. He said fixing youth sports was one of the most important
things anyone could do. I realized Mike, who became founding Chair of
the PCA-Phoenix Chapter, was right, and I was wrong.

The Symbolic Power of Sports

Sports has immense symbolic power. A quarter of most newspapers are
devoted to sports. *Washington Post* sports writer Thomas Boswell argues
that sport "has become central to what remains of our American sense of
identity" and "the meeting ground where we discuss our values."

Millions of people passionately follow elite sports, and what happens
there trickles (or floods) into youth sports. When professional hockey
devolves into violence or a football coach pays bounties for injuring
opponents, those acts are not confined to the pro sports arena; they
reverberate throughout society, which intensifies the need to get sports
right so it enhances, rather than degrades, our world.

The Origins of Positive Coaching Alliance

My first job was working with emotionally-disturbed, behavior-problem kids at the Behavioral Learning Center (BLC) in St. Paul, Minnesota. School leaders Shirley Pearl and Don Challman advocated a relentlessly positive approach, which caused these troubled kids to bloom like plants watered after a long dry spell. I saw firsthand the power of positivity in changing kids' lives.

Later, when my son began playing sports, I was stunned to see kids crying at tee-ball practices because their parents were dissatisfied with their performance, and I was repulsed by a nasty, snarly style of coaching.

The positive techniques I learned at the BLC worked as well with my teams as they had with deeply troubled kids. I wrote *Positive Coaching* and coached the Fremont High girls' basketball team (described in my earlier book, *Shooting in the Dark*).

Along the way, I realized that great coaches weren't enough. An organizational approach was needed. I evolved from sports parent to coach to youth sports leader. I joined the board of Cupertino National Little League, and I started a basketball league.

The Cupertino Hoops Experience

Paul Solomon and I started Cupertino Hoops nearly 25 years ago. We didn't have the Development Zone™ language of this book, but that's what we were after.

We recruited special needs athletes to play beside "normal" kids and future college stars so they could learn from each other. We made the league co-ed, so talented girls could be challenged playing against boys, and so boys and girls could benefit from working together as equals. We obsessively strove to balance teams to avoid blowout games, to the point of moving players after an early season "jamboree" showed us where team imbalances existed. We required every coach to be trained as a "positive coach" in a curriculum that was a forerunner of current PCA training. We gave coaches a branded Cupertino Hoops polo shirt to remind them that they were on a bigger team even while their teams competed with each other. We surveyed parents and players, honored coaches at an end-of-season luncheon and gave them feedback from their players and parents.

And Cupertino Hoops grew because parents loved watching their kids have fun with positive coaches.

A Calling

But even at this point it didn't dawn on me that this might be my calling until John Gardner helped me get appointed to a national task force on Building Character Through Sports. On the flight to Washington, D.C. for the final task force meeting I realized that the report I had drafted was destined to sit on a shelf. I realized an organized approach was necessary to change youth sports. *If I was going to have impact, I needed to be all in.*

My Stanford MBA curriculum had introduced me to the power of organizational culture. When I analyzed youth sports, I saw that sports in our society had become an entertainment culture in which a "win-at-all-cost" mentality predominated.

Still, I had limited ambitions. I just wanted to keep adults from driving kids out of sports. But there was so much more to it, as I discovered.

A Vast Potential

Kids love sports. And they learn early that adults care a lot about how they perform. Because winning can seem like a life-or-death affair – while the actual consequences of failure are pretty mild – sports provides a perfect space to teach life lessons.

Sports is a virtual classroom for building character with an endless procession of teachable moments – opportunities to teach self-confidence, resiliency, teamwork, empathy, mental toughness, self-control, and respect for others – but only if coaches recognize and seize them.

Forty million youth play sports in the United States, more than any other activity besides school. The infrastructure – fields, gyms, tracks and pools – is in place (although low-income areas have far fewer facilities). Youth attend practice with four million mostly volunteer coaches who work with them multiple times per week. Parents make sacrifices so their children can participate in sports.

All that's lacking is the knowledge and commitment to use sports as a Development Zone in which to develop Better Athletes, Better People. The crucial missing piece is leadership to change the culture of youth sports so the adults involved act as character educators. That's where you come in.

Your Crucial Role

I once spoke to a group of youth sports leaders at Stanford while an executive business program was going on next door:

> The folks next door are getting paid to be here. Our society thinks the work they are doing is more important than the work you are doing. But society is wrong.
>
> If you don't provide superb leadership to your youth sports oganization, who will? Who is going to create an environment in which the future leaders and contributors to our society are going to emerge? The answer often is: "No one." That's why your job is so important.
>
> You don't get paid, it's a lot harder than anyone who hasn't done it could ever imagine, and people take it for granted when you do a great job. But it is one of the most important things you can do, an incredible opportunity to make a difference!

There is no better opportunity to impact the trajectory of kids' lives than by leading a youth sports organization to greatness.

The Purpose and Promise of Youth Sports

Our society faces daunting problems. Too often business and political leaders put narrow interest before the greater good and appeal to their followers' lowest instincts. We desperately need more positive contributors and ethical leaders who call us to our highest selves.

Sports done right can produce Better Athletes, Better People. The template for both is the Triple-Impact Competitor® – an athlete committed to making self, teammates and the game better.

Imagine what our world would be like if we had hundreds of thousands of coaches developing millions of athletes who make themselves better, their family, friends and colleagues better, and our community and world better! That is the purpose and promise of youth sports – to help young people reach their highest potential as individuals and as contributors to society.

Take-Aways

1   Leadership of a youth sports organization is one of the most important roles in our society.

2   High school and YSO leaders can affect the trajectory of a huge number of youth by implementing a program that helps kids become Better Athletes, Better People.

3   Youth sports is a major institution in this country that reverberates throughout our society. Change youth sports, we change the country.

**An invasion of armies can be resisted
but not an idea whose time has come.**

Victor Hugo

CHAPTER ONE

The Development Zone:
An Idea Whose Time Has Come

For several years PCA published a list of the Top 10 and Bottom 10 Moments in Sports. In one year alone we saw:

- A brawl between two teams of 8-year-old hockey players

- A dad hurling his 11-year-old son's wrestling opponent off the mat

- A middle-school lacrosse coach hitting a 13-year-old player in the face

- A dad providing steroids and human growth hormone to his 14-year-old son to help improve his speed skating results

- A woman ticketed for leaving her daughter alongside an interstate highway out of anger at the daughter's performance in a soccer match

And then, while I was writing this chapter, the unthinkable happened – Ricardo Portillo, a soccer official in Utah, died after a blow to the head from a teenaged soccer player.

These high-profile incidents are tips of the iceberg. Those involved with youth sports see the problems regularly in daily actions that don't rate media attention:

- Coaches shaming players for mistakes, bending the rules to win, and missing countless teachable moments while in thrall to a win-at-all-cost mentality.

- Parents undermining coaches by criticizing them in front of their children, treating officials with disrespect for calls against their child's team, putting pressure on their child to live up to their often unrealistic expectations.

■ Athletes dropping out in huge numbers, hazing or otherwise treating teammates disrespectfully, and failing to reach their potential as athletes or as people.

When you compare the promise and potential of youth sports to produce Better Athletes, Better People to what actually happens in youth sports, you begin to understand the distressing degree to which our system of youth sports fails to live up to its potential.

Wrong Culture

The problem is that the dominant culture in sports today is an entertainment sports culture. The goal is to entertain fans, which requires winning, which results in a win-at-all-cost mentality that colors every level of sports in our society.

John Madden said, "Winning is the best deodorant." In the entertainment sports culture, if you win, you can get away with things that won't pass the smell test.

Fortunately, there is a competing vision.

Youth Sports as a Development Zone

Ruben Nieves, PCA's Director of Training, coached the Stanford Men's Volleyball Team to an NCAA title in 1997. His team's practice court was separated from its locker room by a curtain. Ruben referred to players entering the practice court as "going through the curtain." They were leaving the outside world behind to enter a place where the norms of the team were dominant.

He used this to build his team's culture. Every time they went through the curtain, he asked them to think about the kind of team they wanted to be and what they needed to do to become that team.

Ruben was creating what Ronald Rolheiser calls a "symbolic hedge" around his practice space. A physical hedge creates a delineated space with some degree of privacy in a yard or garden that may allow you to relax, experience solitude and generally get away from the impact of the rush of pressures from the larger society. A symbolic hedge similarly creates a delineated space where it is easier to focus on what's really important.

Youth sports desperately needs a symbolic hedge to create a space in which participants grow and flourish as athletes and as people. I call this space a Development Zone.

In a Development Zone, people receive different signals about what's important, they are expected to behave differently than in the outside world, and events that occur within the Development Zone have a different meaning than they do in the larger entertainment sports culture. For example:

- In the entertainment sports culture, an unfavorable call by an official is a travesty deserving of rebuke. In the Development Zone, it becomes an opportunity for athletes to work on resilience.

- In the entertainment sports culture, a coach who keeps weaker athletes on the bench may seem savvy. In the Development Zone, this coach is seen to shortchange his players. In the Development Zone, coaches find ways to get kids into games.

- In the entertainment sports culture, setbacks and mistakes are bad things. In the Development Zone they provide a chance for kids to learn to struggle. Many people think struggle is a bad thing. Struggle is a *good* thing, and there is no better place for kids to learn to struggle, adapt and overcome when things don't go well than high school and youth sports.

- In the entertainment sports culture, a game is defined by the results on the scoreboard. In the Development Zone, the scoreboard is much too crude a measurement of success.

It's not that the scoreboard is unimportant in the Development Zone – it is a key *ingredient* in the recipe for developing Better Athletes, Better People. But it isn't everything or the only thing.

The Good News

There is a movement of thousands of people across the United States working to develop Better Athletes, Better People. Here are just a few examples:

- Dallas Independent School District Athletic Director Jeff Johnson keeps the district's electronic message boards filled with positive coaching messages and has implemented new awards for coaches and athletes doing things the right way.

- Hillsborough County (Tampa, FL) Superintendent of Schools MaryEllen Elia requires PCA training for all coaches and pays them for their time in attending workshops.

- Doug Abrams made community service projects part of the culture of the Central Missouri Eagles Youth Hockey Association, including a benefit game and visits to the kids in the University of Missouri Children's Hospital, and fundraising for victims of tsunamis in Asia and Hurricane Katrina in Louisiana.

- Houston Independent School District Athletic Director Marmion Dambrino requires any athletes ejected from a game to attend PCA training before they return to play. Since requiring PCA Training for all HISD coaches, ejections have plummeted.

- Canterbury School (Fort Wayne, IN) Athletic Director Ken Harkenrider has athletes do pre-game PSAs: "I'm about to play my hardest, and I hope you support us positively." "Honor the Game" is painted into the basketball floor and in games with the school's biggest rival, tickets good for a free bag of popcorn are handed out. When fans get the bag it says, "Better Athletes, Better People."

- "B3 Aquatics is a Double-Goal Coached, USA Swimming club team located on the east side of Cleveland (OH)." This is the first sentence in the "About B3" section of the organization's web site, with positive coaching messages all over the website.

- Niles North High School (Skokie, IL) Athletic Director Karl Costello turned around his sports program by starting a booster club to help finance required early morning positive coaching training for his coaches. He went on to finance similar training in the school's feeder programs to impact kids of all ages throughout Skokie.

- The Forman School (Litchfield, CT) created its own branded Honor-the-Game keychain, which is awarded after every game to a member of the visiting team that "...best represents the very heart and soul of the game."

An Idea Whose Time is Coming

Like Victor Hugo, I believe there is nothing more powerful than an idea whose time has come. But ideas don't haphazardly become inevitable. An idea like transforming youth sports into a Development Zone to develop Better Athletes, Better People becomes inevitable only when enough people become champions of the idea and work hard to make it so.

Fortunately, youth and high school sports leaders across this country are working hard to transform their organizations into Development Zones. As more leaders join them, youth sports as a Development Zone will truly be an idea whose time has come!

Take-Aways

1 Youth sports is a precious, fragile system with the potential to develop Better Athletes, Better People. But currently it is a system that is not living up to that potential.

2 A symbolic hedge around youth sports can create a Development Zone in which everything that happens can be used to achieve the goal of developing Better Athletes, Better People.

3 You can help make youth sports as a Development Zone an idea whose time has come!

The only thing of real importance that leaders do is to create and manage culture.

Edgar Schein
Organizational Culture and Leadership

CHAPTER TWO

The Single-Goal Leader:
Why Organizational Culture Matters Most

In his famous essay, "The Hedgehog and the Fox," Isaiah Berlin wrote, "The fox knows many things, but the hedgehog knows one big thing." Jim Collins in *Good to Great* builds on this to say, "Hedgehogs... simplify a complex world into a single organizing idea, a basic principle or concept that unifies and guides everything."

How to create a Development Zone culture is the "one big thing" that high school and youth sport leaders need to know. It is the organizing principle that unifies everything they do in the course of a day, a season, a year, a career. This one thing is so important that a youth sports leader needs to be what I call a Single-Goal Leader™.

Edgar Schein, a giant in management research and education, in his quote at the beginning of this chapter, asserts that culture matters most. He explains, "We tend to think we can separate strategy from culture, but we fail to notice that in most organizations strategic thinking is deeply colored by tacit assumptions about who they are and what their mission is." It is hard to imagine, for example, employees crisply implementing what needs to be done if the culture doesn't value and reinforce efficient operations.

Management guru Peter Drucker summed it up: "Culture eats strategy for breakfast."

The Way We Do Things Here

Organizational culture, according to Marvin Bower of the management consulting firm McKinsey & Company, is simply, *"The way we do things around here."* Or as we stress at PCA, "The way WE do things HERE."

As a youth sports leader, you can do everything else well, but if you don't get the culture right, you fail. Bald Eagle Sports Camps founder Bob McFarlane says, "You can do a lot of things wrong, but if your culture is solid from the top down, there's a lot more forgiveness for the organizational items that aren't perfect."

Pack Animals

As humans, we like to think of ourselves as independent actors who are the masters of our own fate. We like to think we do what we do because we choose it, not because some group we're part of expects it of us.

But this is largely a myth. Humans are pack animals, and, most of the time, most of us run with the pack. We see this when an entire team of athletes decide to shave their heads, or when adults in a company all dress alike.

This is why YSO leaders need to make their cultural norms – "the way we do things here" – explicit.

What Culture Does

An effective culture does three things.

① **It provides clear signals for how to behave.** When people know how things are supposed to be done, if they want to be part of that organization, they try to do them that way. A strong culture can encourage members to work hard, treat people with respect, and sacrifice to achieve the organization's mission. It can call forth the highest and best from people and make it easier for them to do the right thing.

(2) Culture extends your reach. People in every organization have countless interactions with each other and outsiders that leaders don't see. It's the culture that helps assure that people act in keeping with the organization's values.

(3) Culture makes a leader's job easier. Here's Patrick White, long-time leader of an American Youth Soccer Organization (AYSO) region in Southern California: "I view our work with PCA on shaping our culture as preventive maintenance for our AYSO region. Every incident of misconduct consumes eight to 10 hours of my board's time. This is time that takes away from the critical job of growing our region."

Even More So in Youth Sports

Culture is especially crucial in a youth sports organization, where people's children are involved. The passions enflamed in the cauldron of competition can result in ugly behavior. Even more than leaders of other kinds of organizations, youth sports leaders need to be obsessed with culture.

A company CEO or a nonprofit executive director also needs to focus on culture. But it can be argued that there are other aspects of their jobs that may be more make-or-break. A CEO who makes bad strategic decisions may find that everything else she does right can't compensate for that shortcoming. A nonprofit leader who is unable to raise money may find that all the other things he does right are for naught.

But with YSO leaders there is nothing more crucial to success than the culture they establish and defend. Your coaches and parents follow professional and college sports, they read the sports pages every day, they listen to sports talk radio and they keep track of their favorite teams. Without realizing it, they tend to see youth sports through the lens of the entertainment sports culture, bringing to your organization those same assumptions and values.

They are immersed in a culture of sports where winning is everything, and athletes and teams that fail to win are losers, even if they are among the best in the world.

And that means, sooner or later, you are going to have explosions of negativity and win-at-all-cost behavior (WAAC). It may be a coach who humiliates players when they lose. It may be parents who go off on an official who makes a call against their child's team. And it can result in violence. Although you may go a long time without experiencing it, here is something you can count on:

> *If you don't shape a Development Zone culture in your organization, sooner or later the larger WAAC culture will rise up and bite you.*

But you can create a culture that helps coaches and parents see the bigger picture of what youth sports can be. You have that power – *if you will use it.* Coaches need a place to coach. Sports parents need a place for their kids to play. That gives you leverage to implement a Development Zone culture.

What Sports Parents Want

There really is just one thing sports parents – who are, in one sense, your "customers" – want from you. They want the best possible experience for their children. However, they often confuse that with winning.

But with concerted effort, you can teach them that a good sports experience is also about the kind of person their child becomes. You can convince them that your child will get better as an athlete and as a person in your program.

The single, overriding goal for a school or YSO leader – a Single-Goal Leader – has to be to create a Development Zone culture in which Better Athletes and Better People are created. The rest of this book outlines how to do just that.

Take-Aways

1 Culture is simply "The way *we* do things *here*."

2 Culture gives coaches, parents and athletes signals for how to behave, it makes your life easier by preempting many avoidable conflicts, and it extends your reach by encouraging behavior aligned with the organization's values, even when you are not present.

3 If you successfully shape a positive culture, people will forgive many other failings. If you don't, sooner or later the larger win-at-all-cost culture will rise up and bite you.

4 The most important thing a high school or youth sports leader can do is to be a Single-Goal Leader who creates a Development Zone culture where developing Better Athletes, Better People is the paramount goal.

3

**Few, if any, forces in human affairs
are as powerful as shared vision.**
Peter Senge, *The Fifth Discipline*

CHAPTER THREE

The Power of Shared Vision:
A Sense of Possibility for Youth Sports

In March 2000, PCA and the Center for Sport, Character and Culture
at the University of Notre Dame invited 50 youth sports leaders from
around the country to the first annual Against the Grain Forum at
Stanford University.

We had high hopes, but things got off-course early in the two-day
session due to a fierce disagreement about playing time. One person
argued that playing time should be guaranteed for players at every level
of competition, to which the head of a major state high school association took heated exception. We immediately saw that this disagreement
could derail our entire effort.

We called a break, during which we realized we had to agree on a vision
of what youth sports could be like before tackling details like playing
time. We brainstormed for two hours about what such a vision would
look like. Then PCA's Tina Syer drafted a vision statement that began,
"Bottom line, we want to create a culture where kids love to play the
game. They look forward to practices and games as times when they will
have fun. The joy of playing will last a lifetime."

The Vision Statement became a shared vision of the group who attend-
ed Against the Grain, including the two playing-time adversaries!

A Sense of Possibility

Vision is exciting because vision can cause people to act. Vision is not
complicated – it is simply a sense of possibility. In any situation – no
matter how dire – it is possible that things can be improved, sometimes

dramatically, if we can only see it. Being able to sense the possibility – and convince others of it – is a key leadership skill.

The lack of a shared vision can derail efforts before they begin just as it almost did at our Against The Grain Forum. But with an exciting sense of possibility, people step forward to help make it a reality. There are few situations in our society where a lone-wolf approach will succeed. You need collaborators to buy into your vision, to get excited about its sense of possibility.

The Vision of the Development Zone

PCA thinks the phrase that best sums up the sense of possibility for youth sports is "Better Athletes, Better People," which is why PCA adopted it as our tag line. In the Development Zone the roles of key players are transformed. Here's how the key players in youth sports behave in the Development Zone.

The Double-Goal Coach

Each Coach is a Double-Goal Coach®, with one goal of winning and the second, more important goal of teaching life lessons through sports. As Phil Jackson, PCA's national spokesperson, has said, "Not only is there more to life than basketball. There's more to basketball than basketball."

The ROOTS of Honoring the Game are paramount for a Double-Goal Coach:

> **R**ules – Don't bend the rules to win even if you can get away with it
>
> **O**pponents – A gift that pushes you to get better
>
> **O**fficials – Show respect even when they make a mistake
>
> **T**eammates – Never embarrass them on or off the field
>
> **S**elf – This is the foundation. You Honor the Game to live up to your internal standards regardless of external expectations or other people's behavior.

Coaches coach for mastery using the ELM Tree of Mastery (E for Effort, L for Learning, M for bouncing back from Mistakes) and encourage athletes to give their best effort and work through mistakes and failure. They encourage players to develop a Teachable Spirit. They fill players' Emotional Tanks with positive reinforcement for effort and every little bit of improvement.

They see themselves as colleagues with other coaches on a larger organizational team, developing Better Athletes, Better People. They try hard to win, but they never forget that the athletes on other teams are also members of our larger community. They want to see them succeed as well, even in travel play, where opponents are not necessarily part of the same organization.

The Second-Goal Parent

Each Parent is a Second-Goal Parent® who leaves the scoreboard to coaches and athletes while focusing relentlessly on the life lessons a child takes away from sports.

Parents are their kids' biggest fans, and they let them know they believe in them and are behind them no matter how they perform (which makes it more likely that the children will perform well). They behave well when officials make calls against their child's team, or when their child's coach makes a disagreeable decision. On occasion they even cheer good plays by the other team. Because they understand the scoreboard belongs to athletes and coaches, what happens on the playing field doesn't rile them. Because of all this, their children actually like having their parents watch them play!

The Triple-Impact Competitor

Each Athlete is a Triple-Impact Competitor, committed to impacting sport on three levels by improving oneself, teammates and the game as a whole.

Athletes enjoy the challenge of competing, and they can hardly wait to go to practice. They work hard and don't get discouraged easily. They support their teammates even in the face of costly mistakes. They show respect for their opponents and for the officials. They look forward to their own "Mallory Moment"* to elevate the game by the way they compete.

The Triple-Impact Competitor model is a template for Better People as well – Triple-Impact *Citizens* who make our entire society better. The PCA-Houston Chapter annually honors a business leader who exemplifies PCA's Triple-Impact Competitor model in his or her professional and personal life.

The Perfect Game

The perfect Game is closely contested and often decided at the last moment. Each team feels it has a chance to win throughout the game, right up to the last play. All players feel like they have given their all during the game, and they feel proud of how hard they tried whether they won or lost. They feel positive about their opponents and thank them for a great game when it is over.

In the Development Zone, sports can produce Better Athletes, Better People. But simply articulating a sense of possibility is not enough. People have to believe it can happen, and that requires leadership, which I'll address in the next chapter.

---

* The original Mallory Moment occurred on April 26, 2008, when Mallory Holtman and a Central Washington University teammate carried Western Oregon University's Sara Tucholsky around the bases when she injured herself and was unable to complete the home run she hit. This iconic act was recognized by ESPN in its ESPY Awards as the ESPY Moment of the Year. It inspired PCA to challenge coaches and athletes to elevate the game when their own "Mallory Moment" arrives.

Take-Aways

1   Vision is simply a sense of possibility, and *shared vision* is a powerful force for change!

2   The vision of youth sports as a Development Zone includes coaches as a Double-Goal Coach, sports parents as a Second-Goal Parent, and athletes as a Triple-Impact Competitor.

3   The Triple-Impact Competitor is a definition that works for both Better Athletes and for Better People. The former makes self, teammates and the game better. The latter makes self better; friends, family and co-workers better; and our entire society better.

Leadership is the release of energy.
John W. Gardner
Author of *On Leadership*

CHAPTER FOUR

Are You Leader Enough?
Leadership as Emotional Commitment

I know many effective leaders who don't consider themselves leaders at all, partly because we tend to think there is a leadership mold: a leader looks and behaves a certain way. In our society this often means a tall, good-looking, white male who is articulate and charismatic. The thinking is that if you don't fit the mold (and how many of us do?), you really can't be a leader.

But leadership is simply the release of energy to get important work done. One's height, skin color, gender and attractiveness are usually irrelevant to actually getting important work done. Even articulateness can be overrated. The real currency of an effective leader is Emotional Commitment to achieving a vision.

Eugene J. Webb, author of *Unobtrusive Measures* and a mentor of mine at the Stanford Graduate School of Business, used to say, "You can smell emotional commitment a mile away." Your emotional commitment draws the commitment of others. If you have a strong emotional commitment to achieving a goal, and you get people to help you do it, you are a leader. It's that simple.

Leadership is a team sport. Although the solitary leader is a staple in our society's mythology, great organizations usually have a strong leadership team. There are few things of importance that a lone individual can do alone. You have to put together a leadership team that shares your emotional commitment to developing Better Athletes, Better People to give yourself the best chance to succeed.

What Leadership Mostly Is

John Gardner once said to me, "Leadership is mostly teaching and selling. If you're not teaching, if you're not selling, you're not leading."

Compare teach-and-sell with many would-be leaders who "preach-and-tell." They get so wound up in their message that they end up preaching a sermon rather than engaging in a conversation. Great teachers engage people in conversations because it is usually conversations with people we respect that lead to insight and change and even, at times, to transformation.

Would-be leaders also often *tell* people what they should do rather than selling. Selling involves asking questions and listening carefully to identify the overlap between a person's goals and your products or services. Interestingly, engagement and listening seem to come more easily to women than men, which is why I think many women are natural leaders.

Share your passion in a way that leaves room for others to also share theirs. When I first asked Jim Perry, a hall-of-fame coach and athletic director from Southern California, if he would get involved with PCA, he said, "As important as this is to you, that's how important it is to me." Jim's passion for using sports to develop Better Athletes, Better People, along with his talent for inspiring others, has resulted in him becoming one of PCA's finest Trainers, someone we send all over the country and even abroad to spread the PCA Movement.

Relentlessly Fill Emotional Tanks

Recognition is a major leadership task.

We teach coaches that filling the Emotional Tanks of their players is one of their most important tasks. The E-Tank is like the gas tank of a car – if it's low you're not going to go very far. When players' E-Tanks are regularly filled, they end up doing things that even they didn't know they could do.

It's as important to fill adults' Emotional Tanks. Most adults get recognized so infrequently at work or home that if you recognize them, they deeply appreciate it, and it energizes them. We all have so many stresses, so many disappointments, so many tasks that we have to get done with little or no recognition, that our E-Tanks are often near empty. Make a commitment that it will be different in your organization.

Here are two actions to fill your leadership team's E-Tanks regularly:

- **Become a Noticer:** When you look for them, you see appreciation-worthy things all throughout your life. But you have to look, and then take the time and make the effort to recognize people for them. Become a "Noticer" of the helpful things people do, and recognize them for their contributions.

  It's great to tell people directly that you appreciate their hard work. Also use what I call "Third-Party Recognition:" tell someone how much you appreciate someone else's contribution. You will find that your comments often find their way back to the person who did the work. In some ways, it's more of a Tank-filler when a third party lets you know that your boss (or co-worker or spouse or friend) was praising you to them.

  Keep a list of things you notice each week that you want to thank people for. Recognition is one of the most important things you can do as a leader, so don't leave this to chance – keep a list and make it a habit to tell people how much you appreciate their contributions.

- **Appreciations & Triumphs:** We open the floor at PCA staff and board meetings to anyone who has appreciations or triumphs to share. This part of the meeting can go on for 15 minutes or more as people have gotten used to keeping track of how others have helped them, and they enjoy sharing these stories.

  Beginning your meetings with a flood of positivity will result in a team of people with full E-Tanks who are emotionally equipped to tackle tough problems.

It may take people time to embrace appreciations and triumphs, so remember that even if people aren't visibly pleased at being recognized, they are soaking it in like a hot bath, and keep at it.

Fill E-Tanks relentlessly. It may be your most powerful leadership tool to develop an effective leadership team that shares your Emotional Commitment to the vision.

Take-Aways

1 Leadership is the release of energy. Your Emotional Commitment is what draws the Emotional Commitment of others and releases their energy for your shared vision.

2 Leadership is a team sport. Recruit people to your leadership team who can help you achieve your vision.

3 Leadership is mostly teach-and-sell (rather than preach-and-tell). Engage and listen. Share your passion in a way that leaves room for others to express their passion.

4 Recognition is a major leadership task and a powerful tool to develop an effective leadership team. Become a Noticer and relentlessly fill the Emotional Tanks of people in your organization.

It is through conversations – talk, observed
actions, listening, writing – that leaders
manage, reinforce and create culture.

Lisa Haneberg
Author and Management Consultant

5

The Mechanics and Prerequisites of Culture: Creating Your Development Zone

Every organization has a culture – a way of doing things – but often it is slipshod and inconsistent, poorly conceived and unevenly implemented. Great organizations have consistent cultures with clear norms and expectations for behavior that encourage and reward people for doing the right thing at the right time.

Organizational Culture in the Business World

A new CEO may be brought in to turn around a company doing poorly. Perhaps the CEO finds a significant lack of care for customers. The CEO takes steps to integrate customer service into the company's culture to be able to gain enthusiastic repeat customers.

The CEO can't individually manage each employee. But she can manage the organization's culture so people know what they are supposed to do. Some employees may disagree with the new ways and may leave the company, which may be necessary. For the culture to succeed, it's necessary to get the wrong people "off the bus," which we'll discuss later in this chapter.

On the other hand, if employees who embrace this idea and take good care of customers get rewarded, they will be motivated to do more of it. Taking special care with customers eventually becomes just the way this company does things. And, that simple – but not easy – cultural change can transform the failing company into a thriving one.

The same mechanics that leaders of great companies use to establish and maintain a strong, positive culture can be used by youth sports leaders to help their organizations achieve greatness.

The Stages of Culture Shaping

The three stages of developing organizational culture are:

(1) **"Setting the Table"** so everyone clearly understands what kind of behavior is expected in various situations.

(2) **"Fixing Broken Windows,"** in which organization leaders (and eventually others, too) intervene to protect the culture whenever it is violated. People being people, violations will occur, so it is important to have a procedure in place to protect the culture.

(3) Integrate the culture into the **"Structural Pillars"** of the organization so the culture doesn't erode over time. The structural pillars must reinforce the culture through the day-to-day operations of the organization.

In the next three chapters, we'll explore each stage in detail, but first I want to address some prerequisites for establishing a strong culture.

Alignment Before Empowerment

In *The Fifth Discipline*, Peter Senge stresses the importance of getting people aligned with a vision before empowering them. In a typical YSO, people's motives differ greatly – some are there to help kids have a good experience, some to make sure their child gets fair treatment, while others may be living out their own unfulfilled dreams of greatness.

If the leaders empower these unaligned people, things can get ugly. Many YSOs are run by volunteers, and it can be hard to find coaches, so it feels impossible to make demands of them. In effect, the leaders say to the coaches, "Here's your roster, practice times, uniforms and equipment. Now go out and coach the way you coach (whatever that is)."

Get people aligned first, especially coaches: "In this organization we expect every coach to be a Double-Goal Coach who uses practices and games to develop each player into a Triple-Impact Competitor, committed to improving oneself, teammates and the game. The way we do things here, we provide training you'll need to attend so you know how we coach here. No exceptions." (Note: PCA developed on-line courses to make it easier to require Double-Goal Coach training.)

Who Gets On Your Bus – Assembling Your Leadership Team

Jim Collins in *Good to Great* uses the metaphor of a bus: "…if you have the right people on the bus, the problem of how to motivate and manage people largely goes away. The right people…will be self-motivated by the inner drive…to be part of creating something great."

Many people will get excited about the vision of your organization as a Development Zone. You will find that some people, whether they know it or not, have been waiting for someone to articulate this exact concept for a very long time.

But some people will be immune to the vision. They can be a drag on you accomplishing it. And this brings us to a crucial point – not everyone involved with an organization is going to get with your vision of greatness. Sometimes this means some folks need to "get off the bus" for the vision to become a reality.

It's also important to exclude Emotional Tank drainers from your leadership team so they don't drive away the people you want to keep on your bus. Changing the culture of a major institution like youth sports is hard work. You need E-Tank fillers on your team.

To set yourself up for success, you will need two things:

- **A Critical Mass:** You'll never get everyone on board, which isn't necessary, anyway. But you do need a critical mass of people on your leadership team who are committed to the vision. Having people on the leadership team who actively undercut the vision will doom it.

In particular, look for "mavens," individuals who command other people's attention and admiration. (The old commercial comes to mind: "When E. F. Hutton talks, people listen.") Often, mavens are established coaches with a lot of scoreboard success. If you get mavens to be vocal supporters, you are on your way to success.

- **A "Culture Shaping Team:"** To make this work, assemble a Culture Shaping Team (CST) of individuals who see this as the most important thing they can do to make the organization great. It doesn't work so well if it's just you. The CST needs at least two people, preferably three to seven, depending on the size of your organization and its leadership team. Consider carefully who would be excited and effective in this role and recruit them to be part of it. I'll talk in more detail about the CST in Chapter 9.

When individuals in an organization are empowered after they have been aligned with the vision, you have an organization that is ready to take off and do great things!

Who Gets On Your Bus – Recruiting Double-Goal Coaches

After you and your leadership team of culture shapers, the most influential people in your organizations are your coaches. If each of them is a Double-Goal Coach, good things are in store for your athletes. If you have win-at-all-cost (WAAC) coaches, then you are going to have problems.

So it is worth a lot of your thought and energy to figure out how to get the right coaches on your bus and keep the wrong ones off (or help them off if they won't change).

Robert Lewis, Jr., founder of the Boston Astros youth baseball program (now The BASE), tells of an Astros coach who yelled at his players even though he knew that was not the way the Astros did things. When Robert took issue, the coach said, "That's my style." To which Robert replied, "You know, you're right. That is your style, and it just doesn't work for us, so we're going to let you go."

We'll talk about how to align the people in your organization – especially coaches and parents – in the next three chapters. For now, understand that you should articulate a vision of where you want your organization to be, get people on your team who share that vision, and get those who do not share your vision off your bus.

Take-Aways

1 The stages of establishing culture are:

a) Setting the Table so everyone knows what behavior is expected,

b) Fixing Broken Windows by intervening when someone violates the culture, and

c) Building culture into the organization's Structural Pillars so the culture is reinforced over time.

2 Ensure alignment before empowerment! Make sure you have the right people on your leadership team – people who are excited about the vision and who will work hard to make it happen.

3 Exclude Emotional-Tank drainers from the leadership team so they don't drive off people you want to keep on your bus. Changing the culture of a major institution like youth sports is hard work. You need E-Tank fillers on your team.

4 Coaches are hugely influential, the key conduits to the ultimate beneficiary of your Development Zone – the youth athletes. It is crucial to get the right coaches on your bus – Double-Goal Coaches, who understand what it means to coach in the Development Zone – and to get coaches who will not buy into the program off the bus.

They have to hear the jingle seven times
before they buy the toothpaste.

Advertising Industry Lore

CHAPTER SIX

Setting the Table:
Establishing Your Culture

Dinner at the White House

As a member of the board of Special Olympics International, I was
invited to dinner at the White House for the annual taping of "A Very
Special Christmas." I rented a tuxedo, read carefully all the protocol
and instructions I was sent, and worried about which silverware to use
when. I looked around at what others were doing to try to figure out the
"right" behavior.

Contrast this with going to my favorite falafel place. There I don't worry
so much about what I am wearing or my table manners (which hope-
fully wouldn't embarrass my mom!) or if I am acting exactly the way
others are acting.

The way you "Set the Table" helps determine how people behave. And
this is the first step in creating the culture of a Development Zone in
your sports organization.

Message Bombardment

Have you ever watched TV and seen the same commercial three or four
times in a short span of time? A marketing executive in an advertising
class I took at the Stanford Business School explained why this happens:
"They have to hear the jingle seven times before they buy the toothpaste."

People need to hear the same message again and again to become
comfortable with a product, especially a new one. Even if a potential
customer gets bored or upset with seeing the same ad repeated, the

company is willing to risk that in order to get the brand identification and validation that is so important.

At PCA we call this "message bombardment," the key Table-Setting tool to establish with crystal clarity the expected behaviors in your organization. Effectively Setting the Table means that immediately upon contact at *any* point with your organization, people get a Development Zone message that helps them understand when entering your gym, field, track or pool that things are different here. Being bombarded with Development Zone messaging reinforces the idea that all who enter must behave differently (and more honorably) than at a professional sports event.

Setting-the-Table Tools

Here are some practical tools you can use to Set the Table for your organization:

- **Signage:** Coaches, parents and athletes spend a lot of time at fields and facilities. The right signage lets people know they are entering a Development Zone. During lulls in the action, signage also reminds them of the norms of behavior for your organization. For example, Strake Jesuit College Preparatory in Houston prints "Honor the Game" on tickets for football and basketball games. Seeing your messages every time people look around at events is an effective form of passive message bombardment.

  PCA has developed a variety of messages suitable for posting around fields, gyms, tracks and pools (i.e., "We Honor the Game Here" and "Help Our Athletes Excel – Fill Emotional Tanks" and "The ELM Tree of Mastery: Effort, Learning, Mistakes"). Use PCA signs or make your own, but use the message-bombardment power of signage.

- **Handouts:** PCA has developed Honor-the-Game cards, buttons and stickers which are great for special events (see below) but also for everyday situations in which tempers may flare. PCA also developed lollipops ("Positive Parent Pops") branded with "Honor The

Game" to give to parents whose mouths were about to cause trouble. Lollipops make it hard to yell and can last the duration of a competition.

- **Spoken Word:** You typically hear about the need for sportsmanship at the beginning of a season. The organization's leader mentions it at the first meeting of the year, and then you don't hear much about it until the beginning of the next year. Single-Goal Leaders take every opportunity to reinforce the culture with specific examples of the kind of behavior expected:

  ✓ Coaches coming to get their practice schedules? Great! Take two minutes and tell them about the importance of Honoring the Game.

  ✓ Parents here to sign their kids up? Terrific! Take two minutes to remind them about the importance of their filling their child's Emotional Tank.

  ✓ Beginning of a board meeting? Wonderful! Review the importance of the Development Zone culture in developing Better Athletes, Better People.

  Anytime you have leaders, coaches, parents or athletes together and you don't reinforce the Development Zone culture, you have wasted a valuable opportunity.

- **Written Word:** Take advantage of every communication vehicle at your disposal. When people come to your website, they should immediately see messaging consistent with your vision for your organization.

  Send written encouragement through newsletters, e-mail and social media. As the season progresses, the increasing heat of competition can provoke people to do things they will later regret. Regularly reminding coaches and parents about the Development Zone and reiterating your expectations for behavior can prevent or temper such eruptions.

  Bruce Horowitz, founder of Beverly Hills Basketball League, created a series of e-mails called "2-Minute Drills" with PCA messaging that every coach and parent in his league receives weekly. You can create your own messaging, forward PCA's *Momentum* or *2-Minute Drills* (title borrowed with permission from Bruce and BHBL), or both. The important thing is to keep the message bombardment going throughout the season.

Highlight behavior you want to see. When a coach acts graciously to an opponent, tell everyone about it. This reinforces good behavior, reminds everyone of your expectations and plants a seed in the minds of other coaches that they might be recognized if they follow suit.

■ **Gear:** In the first few years of PCA's "Silicon Valley Shootout" basketball tournament, players on corporate sponsored teams talked trash, badgered the refs and even, on occasion, nearly came to blows with each other.

We put "Honor the Game" on every jersey so everywhere players looked they saw the message. This made an immediate difference. We still had players lose their cool in the heat of competition but much less often. And even then, others were quick to say, "Hey, remember to Honor the Game!" And they did!

Annually, every Beverly Hills Basketball League participant gets a newly designed t-shirt with "Honor the Game" on it. Some YSOs put the PCA logo or Honoring the Game on game uniforms sleeves. At Cupertino Hoops, every coach received a navy blue Cupertino Hoops-branded polo shirt to reinforce the idea that they are on the same team working together to develop Better Athletes, Better People.

■ **Events:** Here are two events developed by PCA leaders that help Set the Table.

Honor-the-Game Day was created by Bob Posner of Scotts Valley Soccer and has been used by many PCA Partners at the beginning of the season. Before each contest the officials call the teams together, and the coaches read aloud a statement of their commitment to Honor the Game. Athletes prominently wear Honor-the-Game stickers and distribute Honor-the-Game cards and buttons to their parents, making sure they actually wear the button.

This results in better behavior, and parents, coaches and athletes all get the message that they are expected to Honor the Game. A youth official at the very first Honor the Game Day said, "The parents have been quieter than usual today. Usually, they yell at me and tell me that I called something incorrectly, but they are acting differently today. It is easier for me to concentrate on the game."

Rivalry to Be Proud Of is a great event for high school rivals, especially when there is a tendency for behavior to get out of hand. The ideal situation is to create customized versions of Honor-the-Game cards, buttons and stickers with both schools' logos and colors and distribute them at the gate. An announcement is made just before the game, letting people know that this is indeed a Rivalry to Be Proud Of and asking them to help keep it that way.

School leaders promote this in the week running up to the big game – meeting with student leaders, the band, the booster club and others to gain their cooperation. More information on implementing Honor-the-Game Day and a Rivalry to Be Proud Of are on the PCA website at www.positivecoach.org/LeadersToolkit.

■ **Coaches Training:** Requiring your coaches to attend PCA training and become certified as a Double-Goal Coach is the single most important action you can take to Set the Table.

Coaches work with athletes every week, they interact regularly with parents, and they either model respect for officials or not. The way they coach may override all else you do to make your organization a Development Zone.

PCA training gives your coaches the Double-Goal Coach framework and practical tools including weekly e-mail "Talking Points" that reinforce the lessons from the training throughout the season. Some coaches will immediately embrace this way of coaching. Other coaches will be slower to adopt but will come around as the Development Zone is established and they realize what a powerful impact they can have on the lives of young athletes. And some will leave your organization because they can't give up a win-at-all-cost mindset – and this is a good thing, for your organization and for your athletes.

Requiring coach training gets people's attention ("They must really believe in this if they require it.") It puts steel behind all the talk. Mandating PCA training for your coaches sends a strong signal about what is important to your organization and is a necessary step in Setting the Table for your organization.

Case Study: Setting the Table at Bald Eagle Sports Camps

PCA Trainer Bob McFarlane started Bald Eagle Sports Camps (BESC) in 2010 as the first PCA-approved sports camp. He built the camp around the Triple-Impact Competitor model. Here's how Bob Sets the Table with message bombardment.

- The first thing parents see on the BESC web site is a message letting them know the camp is affiliated with PCA.

- All advertisements prominently note that every coach is PCA-trained and certified. Coaches go through a Double-Goal Coach workshop every year even if they've done it before.

- When parents first check their child into the camp, they receive a copy of *Positive Sports Parenting*. Many parents thank Bob for the book after reading it.

- The camp t-shirt has "Honoring the Game" on the back so people see that message throughout the day.

- At daily meetings, Bob addresses any issues he has noticed and talks through with the coaches how to respond to them as a Double-Goal Coach.

- Each morning, campers hear a short presentation on how a Triple-Impact Competitor makes self, teammates and the game better. Bob does this the first week but quickly moves to having his coaches deliver this talk.

- At awards ceremonies on Friday, each coach recognizes one camper as the Triple-Impact Competitor of the week. Having heard some of these campers talk about what it means to them to be a Triple-Impact Competitor, I can attest that children as young as eight can internalize the Triple-Impact Competitor model!

Bald Eagle Sports Camps has grown from 180 kids in year one to 368 in its second year to 570 in the third year, with less money spent on advertising as positive word of mouth from parents has kicked in. Bob attributes this impressive growth to the effective culture he and his staff have created at BESC.

Effectively Setting the Table usually takes care of 90 percent or more of the problems plaguing youth sports, but not all of them. In the next chapter, we'll discuss how you deal with violations of the culture, what we call "broken windows."

Take-Aways

1 Setting the Table helps determine how people will behave in your organization.

2 Use message bombardment to shower people in your organization with messages about the norms of your culture. Remember, "They need to hear the jingle seven times before they buy the toothpaste!"

3 The most important first step in Setting the Table is to require all coaches to attend Double-Goal Coach training. This gives them valuable tools and it sends a strong signal of what your organization values.

4 Use signage, handouts, spoken word, written word, gear, and events to reinforce again and again the key norms of your culture so there is absolute clarity about the kind of behavior that is expected in the Development Zone.

> **...public order is a fragile thing, and if you don't fix the first broken window, soon all the windows will be broken.**
> James Q. Wilson
> Author and Scholar

CHAPTER SEVEN

Fixing Broken Windows: Defending Your Culture

Why People Misbehave at Youth Sports Events

When an example of bad youth sports behavior hits the mainstream media, journalists often ask me why the parents or coaches involved act in such an awful way. My first response is, "Because they get away with it."

People act inappropriately at youth sports events because there is no price to pay for acting this way. When parents and coaches can't get away with it, they tend to not act this way.

If people know bad behavior in the Development Zone has consequences, they are much more likely to act appropriately. Effective message bombardment described in Chapter 6 gives people unmistakable signals that their behavior will be noticed.

However, humans tend to be boundary pushers, so we shouldn't expect Setting the Table, even when done exceptionally well, will prevent all misbehavior, especially since we are talking about people's offspring. Intervention will be required to protect your culture when – as it inevitably will – inappropriate behavior occurs.

The Broken Windows Theory of Crime Prevention

Let's say a criminal is looking for a place to do his dastardly deeds. He drives through a neighborhood and sees litter on the ground, graffiti on the walls and broken windows. He may conclude that people in this neighborhood aren't paying attention, that this is a place where he can ply his criminal trade.

Then he drives through another neighborhood where the lawns are carefully manicured, the walls are graffiti-free and no broken windows are visible. He realizes he is much more likely to get caught in a criminal act in this neighborhood. Crime averted.

James Q. Wilson pioneered the "Broken Windows" theory of crime prevention, the idea that keeping a neighborhood in good repair tends to result in less vandalism and crime.

The same dynamic can work for you in creating and maintaining your culture. Let's take a typical broken window in youth sports: a parent yelling at an official over a perceived bad call. If this violation of the culture is not addressed immediately, there will likely be more violations in the near future, so it is important to intervene when windows are broken.

Several years ago I was doing a leadership workshop for a soccer club in the San Francisco Bay Area. One of the leaders of this club mentioned he recently had been at a soccer tournament at which he saw something he had never seen before.

A parent from another club was getting all over the officials. The other parents of players on that team quickly hustled the offending individual off the field away from the game. I asked if he knew what league the team was from and he warmed my heart by saying, "Mustang Soccer," a long-time PCA Partner in Danville, California.

Levels of Intervention

Most of us would oppose someone receiving the death penalty for stealing a loaf of bread. We would likely agree with Gilbert and Sullivan's *The Mikado* and the Ramones: "Let the punishment fit the crime."

PCA has developed a system of progressive intervention to protect the Development Zone, divided into "informal" and "formal" levels. If the violation continues, the level of intervention increases.

Informal Levels: One of the perks I enjoyed working at Hewlett Packard was not having to wear a tie except when hosting a customer visit. Usually no higher-up person needed to enforce this rule – when the host forgot to wear a tie, a co-worker reminded him.

Wearing a tie for a factory visit was simply "the way we do things here" at Hewlett Packard. And if you didn't, someone reminded you because many employees, not just supervisors, supported the culture.

In a strong culture, violations tend to be handled informally. When people act inappropriately, someone, often not an official organization leader, intervenes to let them know their behavior is unacceptable.

Informal levels of intervention do not depend on any official action by the designated leaders of an organization. Any member of the organization can invoke them and, in fact, it often works better when a non-leader intervenes. The ideal person to intervene is someone on the same "side" as the person violating the norm.

(1) Nonverbal Prompt: PCA's Tina Syer was at a college field hockey game where her former Olympic Development Program players were competing. She noticed the father of one player ferociously getting on the officials. She happened to be wearing a PCA Honor the Game button, and without saying a word, she handed it to him. He asked, "If I put this on, does it mean I can't yell at the ref?" She nodded her head. He thought for a moment, then put the button on and was silent the rest of the game.

The theory of cognitive dissonance tells us that people want to appear consistent. As strange as it may seem, if someone is simply wearing a button saying, "Honor the Game," he will tend to match his behavior to conform to the button he is wearing even if he doesn't agree with the button!

Notice that Tina's tactic worked even though there was no Development Zone culture established at this college field hockey game. It works even better when there is an established and well-understood set of norms for how people are to behave. Often, all you have to do with a misbehaving person is to give them a nonverbal reminder, but not always.

(2) **Gentle Verbal Reminder:** Let's say handing out a sticker or card with a message has no impact on the person who is misbehaving. Now it's time to step it up just a bit and give a gentle verbal reminder. "Excuse me, remember we want to be good role models inside the Development Zone and not embarrass our kids."

This is most effective when the person giving the reminder is familiar, such as a parent whose child is on the same team. Such a statement from a parent from the other team might escalate the situation rather than help.

And it's best when this is a reminder of something that is already well understood. You can only remind someone that this behavior is not okay in the Development Zone if you've done a good job Setting the Table. With a culture in place, 90 percent or more of the time steps 1 and 2 will deal effectively with the situation, but not every time.

(3) **Assertive, But Non-Confrontational:** You've tried the nonverbal prompt and the gentle verbal reminder. Now, ideally with a smile on your face, you become more assertive: "Hey, that's not the way we do things here."

This should be done in an as friendly and non-confrontational way as possible. When saying this, make sure not to invade the person's personal space. Stay a few feet away so as to not make him feel threatened. Again, the last thing you want is to escalate the situation.

This may turn into a conversation.

> Violator: "But that was the worst call I've ever seen. It was a travesty!"

> You: "I understand, but remember it's important for us to Honor the Game and give our kids the chance to develop resiliency in the face of a bad call."

You want to avoid escalating the situation, but you also want people to understand that their bad behavior is being noticed and will be addressed. You don't need to do this perfectly, but you do need to do it. If the violator ignores you or becomes belligerent toward you, have the self-discipline to simply walk away. You have done what you needed to do.

The Role of Culture Keepers: The best way to ensure appropriate intervention when violations occur is to establish a system of "Culture Keepers." This involves designating one or two parents on each team to have the "job" of reminding other parents on that team to Honor the Game. See the following chapter for a detailed description of how Culture Keepers can help fix your Broken Windows.

Although a strong program of Setting the Table combined with the first three informal steps will deal with as much as 99 percent of the problems, it doesn't work 100 percent of the time. So you now need to back off the Informal personal confrontation and activate the Formal part of the process. You do not want to push violators to the point where there is a violent or nasty confrontation with you.

Formal Levels: Formal levels of intervention are invoked when the Informal levels have failed. PCA developed the following formal system – with an "Official Warning" and two stages of "Removal" – but you can amend it or develop your own.

(4) **Official Warning:** At this point, the violator needs to be informed in a formal way that his behavior is unacceptable. This can happen one of two ways: you or another official representative of the organization can issue the warning. The other way is to work with the officials so they have a system of issuing formal warnings, ideally through the coach of the violator's team.

It is important to educate and empower game officials in this process. When a parent or other spectator is being belligerent, the official approaches the coach of the team the parent is supporting and lets the coach know that his or her team risks forfeit of the game if the coach is not able to correct the fan behavior. The coach then explains that to the violator as an official warning that the team may forfeit the game and that the violator will be removed.

(5) Self-Removal & Removal: If the violator is still not behaving, you as a designated representative of the organization or a game official must give him the option to remove himself. "Sir, you will need to leave this gymnasium. Until you do, the game will not continue. If you do not remove yourself, we will call the police."

Now none of us want to have to call the police to remove a violator, and this system of levels of intervention is designed to make that very unlikely. However, if a violator persists through all the levels, you cannot allow that person to harm your culture. So, although calling the police is a last resort, it is a tactic that needs to be an option in your program.

Culture Building: There is another necessary action – using the results of your reaction to negative behavior to build your culture.

(6) Publicize: Social Learning Theory tells us that people in groups learn how to behave by watching what other people do and seeing what happens. Whenever there is a violation of the norms inside the Development Zone, it's important to let people know that this behavior was challenged rather than ignored.

Publicize the fact that there was a violation and that organization leaders acted to deal with it. Without mentioning names, explain what happened, for example, via e-mail to your organization's members:

"Last week a parent became belligerent at an official's call at a game. He refused to act the way we expect in our culture. Unfortunately, we had to ask this person to remove himself. He will not be allowed back to any of our games until he has shown that he can act in a way that ensures the integrity of our Development Zone which is, as you know, about developing Better Athletes, Better People."

Dealing with Ambiguity – The Traffic Light

Sometimes you just don't know how to handle a situation. Consider the following. The coach of a U-11 baseball team has his pitcher intentionally walk a strong hitter to pitch to a handicapped youth who proceeds to break down in tears after striking out for the last out of the game. This triggers widespread outrage even though intentional walks are legal in this league. What should the leaders of the organization do?

PCA developed the "Traffic Light" to deal with ambiguous situations like this. When something happens that you definitely don't want to happen again, give it a Red Light. Prohibit it and change the rules. Personally, I think intentional walks have no place in youth baseball until about high school.

You could also Green Light it: "The rules allow this. And, although this was unfortunate, intentional walks are part of baseball."

If you don't know how you feel about it, Yellow Light it: "We aren't happy with this, but we're not sure we want to ban intentional walks. So we'll monitor to see if this kind of thing happens again. If it does, we may decide to change the rule."

The Traffic Light allows you to *not* have to respond when you're not sure what the best action is. In many cases, no action will be required in the future because this problem simply won't come up again. If it does, you can act then.

The Bottom Line

The importance of a *system* of graduated intervention cannot be overstated. As Beverly Hills Basketball League founder Bruce Horowitz warns, "If you don't enforce your culture, people will see very quickly that you don't mean business." And that means a Development Zone culture that will not survive for long.

Take-Aways

1 If broken windows are not fixed promptly, you get more broken windows. You need a system of intervention to keep violations of the culture from spreading.

2 Use progressive levels of interventions including "Informal" and "Formal" levels. "Let the punishment fit the crime" by dealing with violations in a gradually increasing way.

3 In a strong culture, violations tend to be handled informally. Everyone knows what is expected. And most people support it, so non-leaders help remind violators of how they should behave.

4 Use the power of Social Learning Theory and publicize what is done about violations as a way of letting people in your organization know that violations will be challenged.

**...builders of visionary companies...
concentrate primarily on building an
organization...Their greatest creation is
the company itself and what it stands for.**

Jim Collins and Jerry I. Porras
Built to Last: Successful Habits of Visionary Companies

CHAPTER EIGHT

Structural Pillars:
A Culture Built to Last

All New People

I spoke at the 50th anniversary of Cupertino (CA) National Little
League. I had been on its board of directors when my son played in
CNLL. Now, some years later I found 100 percent turnover – not one
person from my stint on the board remained, or even knew anyone
from that time.

Writer Anne Lamott notes the impermanence of life: "A hundred years
from now? All new people!" In youth sports, it can be all new people in
a handful of years.

Turnover in youth sports organizations is relentless. Therefore, if you
want the culture to prevail over time, it must be built into the organization's "structural pillars."

Structural pillars include operations, activities and rules that become
routine in the organization's daily life. If you get these routine activities
("the way we do things here") to reinforce your vision, you are on the
road to a culture that is, in the words of Jerry Porras and Jim Collins,
"built to last." In effect, the system reinforces itself.

Three key groups of people need continual reinforcement by your
structural pillars: leadership team members, coaches and parents.

Leadership Team Selection and Orientation

There is no more crucial decision than who gets into the inner circle of leadership for your organization. The wrong people can drain your team of energy and enthusiasm, whereas enthusiastic new blood can fuel everyone on the team.

In a non-school organization, your leadership team is likely to come primarily from your board. In a school you will want to recruit administrators, coaches, parents and athletes who are leaders and who can get excited about the Development Zone.

When recruiting new leadership team members, use your vision of your organization as a Development Zone to screen and evaluate them. Have them read Chapter 3 and ask them open-ended questions such as:

- Why is it important for our organization to be a Development Zone?
- What are some ways we could implement this idea in our program?
- What barriers might keep us from developing Better Athletes, Better People?

Asking candidates to respond to the vision signals to them how important this is, and it gives you a chance to see how they respond. It also can actually be a recruiting tool. Many people want to belong to something bigger than themselves, especially an organization with an exciting vision.

Put in place a vetting process in which members of your core leadership team meet with potential new members. People value belonging to organizations that require them to earn their way in. Following a rigorous process to add members makes it more likely that new members will be committed once they are admitted to your inner circle.

Once new people officially join your board or leadership team, reinforce vision alignment in an orientation session. Have them meet other exemplary, committed members of your team so they understand that this is a vision shared by your team. Here are things to cover as part of their orientation.

- Use this book as a jumping off point to discuss how the Development Zone culture works in your organization, especially Chapter 3.

- If you have a mission statement and/or a board or leadership team member job description, give them a copy and discuss it.

- Ask them to take a PCA on-line course if they have not already done so.

Making these leadership team selection and orientation activities part of your organization's structural pillars will go a long way toward maintaining your culture as the people in your organization change over time.

Coach Development Program

Your coaches are the people who will deliver (or not!) the promises of a Development Zone in your organization. For your vision to flourish, you need every coach to be a Double-Goal Coach, developing every athlete as a Triple-Impact Competitor. Here are four steps to create a Coach Development Program to embed Double-Goal Coaching in the structural pillars of your YSO so it will outlast the current leadership.

(1) **Coach Job Description:** Can you imagine a business that doesn't have a job description for its employees? A great company that doesn't make very clear what it expects its employees to do on a day-to-day basis isn't likely to remain great for very long. Yet most schools and YSOs don't give their coaches a job description.

You want to be *very* clear about what you expect of your coaches. For example, if you feel the test of a good coach is that most or all of his or her players return to your organization the following year, make that an explicit part of the expectations.

PCA's Double-Goal Coach job description spells out specific behaviors. Instead of "Be positive," it specifies actions such as "Use a

Team Mistake Ritual (like Flushing Mistakes) to help players quickly rebound from mistakes," and "Use the Buddy System to teach players to fill each others' Emotional Tanks."

Give coaches a copy of the job description (available at www.positive coach.org/LeadersToolkit) and review it with them, in a meeting or individually, so there is no confusion about what you expect of them.

2 Training Tied to Job Description. If a coach doesn't understand how a Team Mistake Ritual works, for example, he's unlikely to implement it. Mandate PCA training that shows exactly how to implement the elements of the job description.

This is a "moment of will" for a YSO Leader. You may fear the consequences of mandating PCA training. But PCA's experience with thousands of YSOs in the past 15 years tells us that requiring PCA training does not drive coaches away. Rather, being a proud PCA partner sends a positive signal to potential coaches and may bring you additional coaches who want to learn to be a character-building coach.

3 Evaluation Tied to Job Description. Michael LeBoeuf has noted: "People do what gets measured." Letting coaches know ahead of time that you will survey their players and their parents on how well they implement Double-Goal Coach practices makes it *much* more likely they will do so.

Regular evaluations will also give you terrific information about your coaches that will come in handy, for example, when a parent complains about his child's coach. Perhaps the coach is at fault. But it is also possible that this is an unreasonable parent. Even if you are visiting practices and games, you may not be able to get beyond parent-says/coach-says.

However, if you conduct a mid-season survey of parents and players, you have hard evidence. If five or six of 12 parents have a problem with the coach, it is likely the coach needs to improve. On the other hand, if all the other parents are happy with the coach's behavior, then the problem may lie with the complaining parent.

Or what if you have some indication that one of your coaches is not living up to your expectations? You have a conversation with him and he says, "How do you know? You aren't at my practices. You don't know how I coach." With survey data you have evidence, which also makes it easier for you to have a hard conversation with the coach.

With evaluation it isn't *you* telling him he's not doing the job, it's the data telling him he needs to improve. "Let's take a look at the job description, and you tell me how you think you are doing with these items." You are there to help him get better so he can get the parents off his back.

While I have reservations about "teaching to the test," there is no question that people work to master what they believe they will be tested on. Therefore, your coaches are much more likely to adopt Double-Goal Coach techniques, knowing that players and parents will be asked about whether they are using them.

(4) **Awards Tied to Evaluation.** Michael LeBoeuf again: "What gets rewarded gets done." Align your awards with desired coaching behavior, and good things will happen.

Recognize coaches who get stellar marks from players and parents. Hold a coach appreciation event to make sure every coach is appreciated while giving an award to deserving coaches for their exemplary coaching. Nominate your best coaches for PCA's national Double-Goal Coach Award Program.

However you decide to honor your top coaches, make sure you spread the word about those being honored (and *why* they are being honored) via e-mail and social media as well as letting the local media know about coaches who win your award. As mentioned in Chapter 7, Social Learning Theory says that people learn what is expected of them by seeing what behavior is rewarded in an organization, so trumpet your winners from the rooftops!

Now do something that will multiply the impact of this award. Buy a large perennial plaque that will name the winners from multiple years. At the beginning of the next season, bring the perennial plaque to every meeting and refer to the coaches whose names are on the plaque so other coaches will think, "I'd kind of like to have my name on that plaque."

As John Gardner once told me, awards programs exist not so much for the few people getting the awards as for the many people who modify their behavior so they might qualify for an award in the future.

Incorporating a Coach Development Program into your structural pillars will create a virtuous cycle in which Positive Coaching behaviors by your coaches will be reinforced and perpetuated long after your current leaders have left the organization.

Recruiting Great Coaches

If you lack enough of the kind of Double-Goal Coaches a Development Zone requires, here are some ideas for recruiting more coaches.

1 Appoint a Recruitment Manager: Find an out-going, sales-oriented individual with determination and persistence to be your Coach Recruitment Manager.

2 Develop Your Message: "This is not just another sports organization. We are part of the Positive Coaching Alliance Movement, and we are looking for coaches who want to develop Better Athletes, Better People. We provide free PCA training, the chance to make a difference in the lives of athletes, and the chance to coach in an organization that Honors the Game."

3 Advertise and Promote: Many local newspapers, online and other media are hungry for content, so provide them with a recruiting notice. Pitch a story to a local editor about the great experience you provide to athletes and coaches.

4 Start Early and Follow Up: Get recruiting notices out well before you will need coaches. Follow up with phone calls to make sure they were received and will run and to see if there is anything else needed. Resubmit your notices every week until you get the coaches you need.

5 Hold Information Sessions: That way, prospective coaches get a chance to check you out.

6 Go Where Potential Coaches Are: Many former high school athletes don't compete in college and might love to coach. Community colleges often have PE or coaching courses. High school athletes may be interested in becoming assistant coaches.

7 Enlist Current Coaches as Recruiters: Experiment with giving current coaches a reward (a hat or the like) for successfully recruiting coaches.

8 Encourage Mothers to Coach: Offering Positive Coaching and skills clinics along with the option of starting as an assistant may allow you to tap into a much larger pool of potential coaches.

9 Evaluate: After the season, ask a focus group of coaches what they appreciate about the organization, what could be improved, and how to get more coaches. Solicit testimonials that can be used for next season's marketing.

Parent Expectation Program

The third group you need to keep aligned with your Development Zone culture is the parents of your athletes.

Sports parents – and remember that I was one for many years – are like toddlers: if you don't find things for them to do, they get into mischief. If you don't find ways for your parents to support your Development Zone culture, they will often undercut it. Here are two key steps to create a Parent Expectation Program that will support your culture.

(1) **Establish Clear Expectations for Parent Behavior:** People aren't likely to do what you want them to do if they don't know what that is. Since the expected behavior for parents in the Development Zone is significantly different than common behavior of fans in the entertainment sports culture, here are some methods for establishing those expectations:

a) **Educate Each of Them on Becoming a Second-Goal Parent:** Getting your parents to a Second-Goal Parent workshop (either live or on-line) is the best way for them to learn the power and possibility of helping their children have a great experience, while supporting and reinforcing the Development Zone culture.

Through years of working with schools and youth sports organizations, we have found that parents are the hardest people to reach. PCA has two live parent workshops and an on-line workshop. We added a 30-minute Parent Talk to our original two-hour Second-Goal Parent Workshop specifically for middle and high schools that could allocate 30 minutes as part of a "back to school" night. It will take work to attract a parent audience, but it is worth the effort. A typical comment on evaluation forms from parents who do attend is, "I didn't want to do this as I thought it would be a waste of time. But now I realize every parent should be required to go through this. It was that helpful."

b) **Books:** Consider giving a copy of PCA's *Positive Sports Parenting* or *The High School Sport Parent* books to your parents. These slim, tool-packed volumes are available in bulk rate. A book is typically part of the live PCA Parent workshop, but if you are not able to have a live workshop, giving the book to your parents, especially parents new to your organization, provides them useful information, lets them know you care about their experience with your organization and lets them know your expectations for their behavior.

c) **Parent/Guardian Letter:** Inform parents via a letter or e-mail what you expect from them. Use PCA's sample letter describing expected behavior or develop your own.

d) **Parent Pledge:** PCA also has a Parent Pledge that asks parents to agree to behave in specific ways that reinforce the Development Zone culture. For example, "I will engage in No-Directions Cheering, limiting my comments during the game to encouraging my child and other players (from both teams)."

The Parent/Guardian Letter, Parent Pledge and many other tools can be found on PCA website at www.positivecoach.org/LeadersToolkit.

(2) **Appoint Sideline Culture Keepers:** Because youth sports involves people's children, setting expectations for behavior isn't enough. Recruit parents to serve as sideline "Culture Keepers" who will reinforce Development Zone behavior on the sideline. Here is the job description for Culture Keepers:

a) Become familiar with PCA principles via a live or on-line workshop, books, Talking Points, newsletters and other web-based resources (www.positivecoach.org).

b) Get to know other parents early each season, explaining the role of Culture Keeper and enlisting their support.

c) Be visible on the sidelines, wearing and distributing Honor the Game buttons, as well as stickers and cards to other parents (all available from PCA).

d) Model desired sideline behavior such as remaining silent after a questionable call and cheering good plays from both teams.

e) Welcome new parents to the program and explain "the way we do things here" in the Development Zone.

f) Remind fans on the sideline to Honor the Game and have fun.

g) Thank and reinforce parents and fans who Honor the Game.

h) Understand the levels of intervention in Chapter 7, and intervene appropriately and safely when parents violate the Development Zone culture.

If you build into your structural pillars the practices described in this chapter, you will find yourself with a culture built to last. The people will change but the vision remains!

Take-Aways

1   With turnover rampant in leadership of youth sports organizations, it's crucial to incorporate your Development Zone culture into the structural pillars of your organization so the system reinforces itself over time.

2   There is no more crucial decision than who gets admitted to the inner circle of your leadership team. Ensure you get individuals who are aligned with your Development Zone vision through a selection and orientation process that verifies their enthusiasm and commitment.

3   Implement a Coach Development Program with job description, training, evaluation and awards for those who excel.

4   Establish clear expectations for parents and recruit one or two from each team to serve as sideline Culture Keepers to reinforce the Development Zone culture.

We define grit as perseverance and passion for long-term goals...The gritty individual approaches achievement as a marathon; his or her advantage is stamina. Whereas disappointment or boredom signals to others that it is time to change trajectory and cut losses, the gritty individual stays the course.

Angela L. Duckworth, et al.

Grit: Perseverance and Passion for Long-Term Goals

CHAPTER NINE

Grit, OPURs and Action Plans: The Art of Implementation

PCA Trainer Billy Pieper uses a football example in the PCA leadership workshop to illustrate how good intentions aren't enough: "All the players huddle around the quarterback who calls a play. But then everyone on the team runs to the sidelines and sits down on the bench!"

Isn't this often what happens with our good intentions? We get fired up to do something great, like create a Development Zone, but then our life responsibilities overwhelm us. And the result, often, is that we go to the sidelines. And nothing happens.

Implementation is Hard

Let me remark on what may be obvious: implementation is hard. As hard as it can be to develop an effective strategy, it is even harder to effectively implement it.

Significant change to any complicated system is difficult and can take time to implement. High school and youth sports involve a large number of coaches, parents and athletes; they are constantly impacted by the larger sports culture; and they arouse visceral, deeply felt emotions. So it is good to realize that changing your organization into a Development Zone is not necessarily going to be easy.

There are many reasons why creating a Development Zone is difficult, which is why effective leadership of a high school or youth sports program requires an Action Plan and the grit – perseverance and passion for long-term goals – to see the plan through.

Individuals with Grit

Some people talk a good game but never seem to get anything done. Other people love to get things done and check things off the many lists they make.

When you look for people to help you implement Action Plans to create a Development Zone in your organization, look for individuals with grit – those who are not comfortable until they have done what they set out to do. If they come up short on occasion, it's only temporary, and they recharge themselves to go back and tackle the difficult, unfinished task again.

Also recognize the need for grit in yourself. Remind yourself from time to time of the importance of your work in developing Better Athletes, Better People and tell yourself, "I'm the kind of person who has the grit to see this through."

The Crucial Role of the OPUR

Tom Peters and Robert Waterman, authors of *In Search of Excellence,* note how difficult it is to change an organization and how it often requires what they call "a monomaniac with a mission."

Jim Collins, whose work on great organizations informs this entire book, says the key to successful implementation is to identify what he calls an "OPUR" (OH-purr) for anything that you really want to have happen.

OPUR stands for the "one person ultimately responsible." That's the person who has publicly committed to make a certain thing happen. Now at the end of a PCA staff meeting, someone will usually say, "Okay, who's the OPUR on this?" Or even better: "I'll be the OPUR on this."

Make OPUR a term that is part of the way you do things in your organization, and try to end every meeting with a summary of the actions needed, including identifying the OPUR for each. Action Plans without identified OPURs are exercises in frustration.

Culture-Shaping Team

As we discussed in Chapter 4, leadership is a team sport. And a team is what you need to create a Development Zone. It *just works better* if you have at least one other person to share your burning commitment for creating a Development Zone culture. Your "Culture-Shaping Team" (CST) should include at least two people (3-7 is often a good size) who will drive your Action Plan.

Identify and recruit individuals to join your Culture Shaping Team who share your burning commitment to create a Development Zone.

- School CSTs should include influential, active parents perhaps from the booster club, "maven" coaches (who other people listen to), representatives from the administration, someone to be the communications OPUR, and don't forget to include student-athlete leaders. Bill McDonald of Strake Jesuit Preparatory in Houston, for example, created an athlete PCA Council that meets regularly to address how to create and maintain a positive culture at the school.

- In non-school YSOs, your CST may be mostly board members who are on fire to do this. But don't overlook people with grit who don't serve on the board; they may see board meetings as a drag, but get excited about getting things done. Again, you will want to have a communications OPUR and include maven coaches.

In Chapter 4 I quoted John Gardner: "Leadership is mostly teaching and selling." Try selling the Development Zone to a few maven coaches – your most influential and successful – and ask those that respond enthusiastically to join the CST. Including maven coaches will make it easier for other, skeptical coaches to buy into the Development Zone culture.

Get on the Agenda

Chuck Hellings of PCA Partner ePath Learning told me: "Human nature dictates that nothing happens until it has to. Leadership is making something happen before it has to."

Over many years of experience with volunteer nonprofit organizations made up of busy people, I observed a phenomenon that has evolved into a rule of thumb: 90 percent of the work in a volunteer organization gets done the day before the next board meeting.

I encourage you to use this phenomenon to your advantage by ensuring that there is always another meeting coming up soon. Make sure the CST is unfailingly on the agenda for every meeting. Knowing they must report on their progress at the next meeting will motivate CST members to complete their tasks so they will have progress to report on.

During CST meetings, always end by identifying the OPUR for every crucial task. And make sure everyone knows when the next meeting is!

The Simplicity of a Good Plan

The key to all of this is the Action Plan. You can develop complicated plans with bells and whistles, but at its core, the effective Action Plan is a simple thing (remember "simple" does not mean "easy"!).

A good Action Plan includes the task, the OPUR, and a time when the task will be done. That's really all you need if you have gritty people working the plan.

The Advantages of a Bad Plan

A story: Soldiers on maneuvers in the winter got lost in the mountains. They became discouraged by the cold and frustrated as the daylight began to diminish. One soldier found a map in his pack and everyone huddled excitedly around him while they figured out where they were. They were filled with renewed energy as they headed back to base camp.

When they arrived, they debriefed their commanding officer who asked to see the map. After examining it for a while he informed them, "This is a map of a different area than you were in."

A bad plan is better than no plan because it can get you motivated and moving, and when you are moving, things can happen that just don't happen when you are stuck in place.

At PCA we live by Anne Lamott's idea of "Crummy First Drafts," from her book, *Bird By Bird*. Desire for perfection can immobilize you. Get the crummy first draft of your Action Plan down on paper. You can then revise it as needed. If you try to develop the perfect plan before you commit it to paper, you will lose valuable time. And it won't be perfect anyway. As Prussian Army Chief of Staff Helmuth von Moltke the Elder noted many years ago: "No plan survives contact with the enemy."

The planning is more important than the plan, because once you start to implement any plan, you will encounter circumstances that you could not have foreseen that compel a change of plans.

What to Do When

In our work with schools and YSOs, we've come to three important conclusions for successful Development Zone Action Plans.

(1) Use Message Bombardment to start with a bang. Your coaches, parents and athletes need to *know* that you are implementing a Development Zone culture. They need to understand how important this is to you and your leadership team, and to the future of their children. So bombard them with Development Zone messages right away so there is no confusion in anyone's mind about what you are going to do.

(2) Use what Karl Weick of the University of Michigan calls "small wins" to build and maintain motivation of your team. Get some things done and recognize people for making them happen. For example, starting a season with an Honor-the-Game Day allows you to involve many people in specific tasks to accomplish a very tangible and visible action that will let everyone in your organization know what a Development Zone culture is and that you are embarking on it. An early Honor-the-Game day also helps you to start with a bang!

(3) Use "Stretch Goals" to find the right balance of tasks to tackle. Set goals that you are confident your team can accomplish, and then challenge yourselves with Stretch Goals that you and your team will have to stretch to be able to accomplish. Stretch Goals motivate high performers who love to be recognized for great accomplishments. And because these goals are by definition "stretch," people with limited time or who may be overwhelmed by too aggressive a goal have the security of the achievable goals to focus on.

The Fog of Planning

When I started PCA, I heard an analogy that sustained me during difficult times when I wasn't sure what to do next: You are driving a car in the mountains at night in a pea-soupy fog. You can barely see three feet in front of your car.

But you can see three feet! And when you keep going, then you can see three feet farther. And then three feet farther. And then once in a while, if you keep at it, the fog will suddenly lift and you can clearly see way down the road to where you want to go!

Implementation is difficult because the world is complicated. But with an Action Plan and a Culture-Shaping Team of gritty individuals who embrace the concept of the OPUR, you absolutely can get through the fog of uncertainty and create a Development Zone in your organization.

Take-Aways

1 Recognize that creating a Development Zone is a marathon rather than a sprint. Tell yourself often, "I'm the kind of person who has the grit to make this happen!"

2 Recruit a Culture-Shaping Team (CST) of gritty individuals who like to make lists and check things off lists.

3 Plan! A bad plan is better than no plan, so get a crummy first draft Action Plan done, understanding that you'll need to revise the plan as you learn more.

4 Identify an OPUR (the One Person Ultimately Responsible) for every important task. Make the OPUR part of your culture (the way we do things here!).

5 Get on the Agenda. Make the Culture-Shaping Team's Development Zone work a regular agenda item for every meeting.

6 Start with a bang. Use Message Bombardment to let everyone know what a Development Zone is and how important it is.

7 Accumulate small wins and use Stretch Goals to keep your team motivated.

10

We are what we repeatedly do.
Excellence, then, is not an act, but a habit.

Aristotle

CHAPTER TEN

The Habit of Excellence:
A SMaC Recipe for High School and Youth Sports Leaders

In *Great By Choice*, Jim Collins coined the term "SMaC Recipe" to help leaders understand what needs to happen for their organizations to become great: "A SMaC Recipe is a set of durable operating practices that create a replicable and consistent success formula." SMaC stands for Specific, Methodical and Consistent.

SMaC, unlike big picture things like developing a vision, is about crucial operational things that – done repeatedly – will make your vision a reality and move your organization toward excellence. A SMaC Recipe can help make these crucial actions an organizational habit ("the way we do things here"). Collins again: "…the signature of mediocrity is not an unwillingness to change; the signature of mediocrity is chronic inconsistency."

Here is an initial Development Zone SMaC Recipe. You may want to add to, subtract from or modify this version to create a customized SMaC Recipe for your organization. Review it regularly to measure your progress in implementing your Development Zone culture.

Development Zone SMaC Recipe

1 Emotionally commit in writing to your Development Zone vision.

- Embrace your role as a Single-Goal Leader. Recognize that creating a Development Zone is one of the most important things you can do in your life.

- Remind yourself that you have the grit to stick with it to make your vision happen by reviewing your written commitment regularly.

- Share your Emotional Commitment with your leadership team.

2 Ensure alignment of your board or leadership team. Implement a vetting process, including meetings with potential leadership team members, to make sure individuals are emotionally committed to the Development Zone vision before they join your team.

3 Form your Culture-Shaping Team (CST) with individuals with the grit to be the drivers of Development Zone implementation.

4 Make sure the CST has Action Plans for the upcoming season with OPURs identified for every crucial task. Make the work of the CST an agenda item for every meeting to spotlight their crucial work and ensure follow-through.

5 Be a noticer. Keep written notes on actions members of your CST and leadership team take to strengthen the Development Zone culture. Use your notes to regularly fill their Emotional Tanks publically during Appreciations & Triumphs time at your meetings as well as letting people know individually.

6 Include funds for training in your budget, and schedule training for your leadership team, coaches, parents and athletes prior to the beginning of the season. If needed, activate a recruiting plan for coaches.

7 Set the table with Message Bombardment.

- Reinforce the Development Zone culture at every point of contact people have with your organization: web site, venue signage, handouts, gear, speeches by organization leaders, newsletters, and regular e-mail messages.

- Hold an Honor-the-Game Day or Rivalry to be Proud Of event early in the season.

8 Fix Broken Windows immediately.

- Nip problems in the bud. Be prepared to jump on any violation of the Development Zone culture before it can get out of hand or lead to a degrading of the culture.

- Use progressive levels of informal and formal interventions to deal with behavior that violates the Development Zone culture.

- Recruit and train parents as Culture Keepers to teach and reinforce the Development Zone culture on the sidelines and in the stands.

9 Implement a Coach Development Program.

- Distribute the Double-Goal Coach job description to every coach.

- Require every coach to be trained and certified annually in Double-Goal Coaching.

- Survey parents and players (ideally in mid-season) on how well your coaches are doing as Double-Goal Coaches.

- Use the feedback from the surveys to help coaches improve.

- Reward coaches who are doing a great job with your own Double-Goal Coach Award. Nominate at least one deserving coach every year for PCA's national Double-Goal Coach Award.

10 Implement a Parent Expectation Program

- Through regular communications via website, e-mail, newsletter, etc., establish clear expectations for your parents to be Second-Goal Parents.

- Encourage or require parents to become trained as a Second-Goal Parent.

- Distribute copies of *Positive Sports Parenting* or *The High School Sports Parent* to your parents.

- Distribute PCA's Parent/Guardian letter and Parent Pledge (or your own version of them) to parents annually.

- Appoint parents as Culture Keepers for each team in your program.

Take-Aways

1 Use a SMaC (Specific, Methodical and Consistent) Recipe – the one in this Chapter or your own – to bring consistency to your organization's Development Zone culture.

2 Review your SMaC Recipe regularly to measure your progress in implementing a Development Zone culture.

11

Tell me, what is it you plan to do with your one wild and precious life?
Mary Oliver
"The Summer Day" — *New and Selected Poems*

Your Legacy

I recently talked with a fellow I know. He was morose, even though it was a lovely day. I asked how it was going, and he said, "Not so well. I really don't know what I've accomplished in my life. You have a legacy with PCA you can be proud of. I don't have that."

As we age, the question of what we have accomplished in our "one wild and precious life" looms larger. The big plans we may have had when we were younger often don't pan out, and we set our sights lower, sometimes much lower.

But if you are involved in leading a youth sports organization, you can create a vision of a Development Zone that can impact the trajectory of a huge number of youth.

There is no mystery to creating a vision. Vision is simply a sense of possibility. I've tried to lay out in this book how you can create a vision of a Development Zone in your organization.

Leadership is also not that complicated – not easy, but not complicated. If you show your emotional commitment to your vision, you will be able to get other people excited about it. If you become a noticer and fill their Emotional Tanks when they contribute, they will enjoy being part of creating a legacy for themselves also.

Legacy is tied to meaning. And for a youth sports leader, as Bruce Horowitz of Beverly Hills Basketball says, "Meaning is having the ability to impact so many lives with an activity that everyone can enjoy." You can make a difference. You can help your organization develop Better Athletes, Better People. Your efforts will be linked to those of many others across the country through the PCA Movement.

And you will have created a legacy of which you can be proud.

Take-Away

Creating a Development Zone that impacts the trajectory of the lives of many youth is a wonderful legacy available to any Single-Goal Leader.

Acknowledgements

Special thanks to the "brain trust" of individuals who contributed to this book: Doug Abrams, Al Adamsen, Cameron Campbell, Andy Crossley, Tom Cassutt, Tom Cecola, Karl Costello, Jeff Dale, Eric Eisendrath, Bob Everett, Michelle Gazarik, Christine Haberman, Ken Harkenrider, Ripper Hatch, Steve Henderson, Bill Herenda, Rich Heritage, Sandra Hietala, Janet Holdsworth, Bruce Horowitz, David Jacobson, Jeff Johnson, Mike Lage, Robert Lewis, Jr., Ray Lokar, Bill McDonald, Bob McFarlane, Dean Munro, Ruben Nieves, Jim Perry, Kiha Pimental, Courtney Pollack, Bob Rhein, Ben Rose, Jason Sacks, Craig Salgado, Scott Secules, David Shapiro, Heana Simpson, John Stamos, Steve Stanford, Cathie Whalen and especially Tina Syer. Thanks also to the entire staff of PCA. Each of you helped make this book possible.

The author is grateful for the many culture and leadership lessons absorbed over many years from Paul Alexander, Dana Bainbridge, David Bradford, Bruce Brown, Bill Campbell, Don Challman, Scott Chapman, Jim Collins, Kevin Compton, Gordon Cosby, Bill Drayton, Mark Edmunds, Joe Ehrmann, Karen Francis, Lynn Frank, Doug Galen, John Gardner, Dick Gould, Irv Grousbeck, Kirk Hanson, Laura Hazlett, Chip Heath, Lucy Heegaard, Nancy Huang, Phil Jackson, Ron (RJ) Jensen, Shane Kim, Steve Knaebel, Rod Kramer, Bill Lazier, Ted Leland, Leo Linbeck III, Jim Lobdell, Art Lovering, Ross Malinowski, Jim March, Wendy McAdam, Bill Meehan, Debra Meyerson, Fred Miller, Mark Murphy, Killian Noe, Elizabeth O'Connor, Jim Patell, Lisle Payne, Shirley Pearl, Gary Petersmeyer, Jeff Pfeffer, Tamar Pichette, Sister Grace Pilon, Walt Pollock, Jerry Porras, Ray Purpur, Leo Redmond, Rodger Rickard, Doc Rivers, Diane Rosenberg, Ralph Rusley, Pulin Sanghvi, Steve Seely, Sargent Shriver, Steve Stenersen, Greg Tehven, Gabriel Thompson, Mike Town, Larry Varellas, Jill Vialet, Gene Webb, David Weekley, Dan Whalen, David White, and Steve Zuckerman.

Workshop Evaluation

Date: _____

PCA Presenter: _____

Your organization or school: _____

Gender: ☐ Male ☐ Female   Your Age: _____

Ethnicity: ☐ White ☐ African-American
(check all
that apply) ☐ Latino ☐ Asian-American ☐ Other: _____

Sports you are representing today: _____

Age group you play/coach/parent: _____

To help us do a better job, we need your feedback. Thank you very much!

		POOR	AVERAGE			EXCELLENT
1.	Overall workshop	1	2	3	4	5
2.	Presenter's effectiveness	1	2	3	4	5
3.	Content of the workshop	1	2	3	4	5
4.	Length of the workshop	☐ Too Short	☐ Just Right		☐ Too Long	

		NOT AT ALL			VERY WELL	
5.	Did your presenter clearly explain PCA's concepts and tools?	1	2	3	4	5
6.	Did your presenter keep you engaged during the workshop?	1	2	3	4	5
7.	Did your presenter effectively respond to participant questions and concerns?	1	2	3	4	5

		DISAGREE			AGREE	
8.	I intend to use workshop ideas this year	1	2	3	4	5
9.	I would recommend others attend this workshop	1	2	3	4	5

10. The best part of this workshop was: _____

_____

11. A way to improve this workshop is: _____

_____

Become a PCA Member Today!

For as little as $25 per year, you can help PCA make a difference in the lives of hundreds of thousands of athletes every year!

As a member, you will be invited to hear podcasts and webinar discussions featuring top athletes and coaches like Summer Sanders, Doc Rivers, and Steve Young. You'll also get a Triple-Impact Competitor Bag Tag to give to a student-athlete!

Yes, I want to make a difference in youth sports by donating:

☐ $25

☐ Other Amount _____

Your Name _____

Street Address _____

City, State, Zip _____

Phone _____

Email _____

☐ Please make my gift anonymous

☐ I/We work for a matching gift company

To sign up online, visit **http://donate.positivecoach.org/Membership**

Or mail this form to:

Positive Coaching Alliance
Attn: Membership
1001 N. Rengstorff Ave., Suite 100
Mountain View, CA 94043